GO Lucy GO!

Part of the Resilient Ratties Series

Giving children the skills to understand and manage their own emotions and mental health

Welcome to the Resilient Ratties Series! Follow Max and Lucy on their adventures whilst learning valuable life skills along the way.

Thank you

I would like to thank my husband Rikki and two children Ellie and Rian for supporting me through this exciting journey of writing children's books!

Thanks also to my Dad, Alex and Catherine (without whom this book would not have been possible) and finally thank you to my amazing Niece Daisy for believing in me and motivating me to keep going with the series.

Thank you from the bottom of my heart to each and every one of you!

me & ginger

ellie & alfie

the boys!
alfie, ralph, ginger & jinx

rian & ralph
(& jinx!)

Notes to adults

As a mental health practitioner for over 12 years, I have been supporting adults to learn skills in order to help manage and maintain their mental and physical well-being. I am so excited to publish the second book in the Resilient Ratties series, introducing both children and adults to more of The Decider Life Skills. These skills have completely transformed not only my practice but also the lives of the individuals that I work with. Time and time again I hear people say *"I wish I had learned these skills years ago..."* and now it's so fantastic to hear the feedback about these books and the real-life skills children are learning from reading them!

I hope you find these books both fun and educational. They have been written and designed to help you learn alongside your child in a way that they can understand, enjoy and remember. You can use the **Learning Together** section at the end of each book to open up conversations and encourage children to learn about how the skills apply to them and their surroundings, whether at home, school or playing outdoors.

Finally... why did I choose to bring the skills to life with my cartoon rats? I have five cheeky ratties of my own! Rats are incredibly misunderstood creatures but once you get to know them, they are extremely intelligent, adaptive and resilient characters who seek social connection and relationships! So why did I choose rats?... Why not!

The Decider
Winning strategies for mental health

About The Decider Life Skills

Giving children the skills to understand and manage their own emotions and mental health

The **Decider Life Skills** were developed in Guernsey by Michelle Ayres and Carol Vivyan, both CBT therapists with a background in mental health nursing. They are a package of 12 individual, evidence-based skills aimed at tolerating distress, regulating emotions, increasing mindfulness and improving relationships. You can find out more information and evidence about The Decider Life Skills including online training, school packages and other resources by visiting their website: **www.thedecider.org.uk** there are also lots of helpful resources on their sister website **www.getselfhelp.co.uk**

First published in UK in 2020 by Fiona Woodhead from FiandBooks.com

67 The Hollins, Triangle, Halifax, West Yorkshire. HX6 3LU.

www.fiandbooks.com

www.fiandbooks.com

ISBN 978-1-909515-10-9

FI & BOOKS BECOME-AN-AUTHOR WINNER 2019

Lucy couldn't stop thinking about the obstacle course that their teacher Mr Chip had planned for after lunch. Lucy's brother Max had already told her about the tunnel in the obstacle course. Max said the tunnel would be scary, long, dark and twisty. Whenever Lucy thought about the tunnel, she noticed different things happening in her body. She could feel butterflies in her belly and her heart beating fast. Lucy recognised the signs that she was feeling her Fizz and that meant she felt scared.

Lucy's Fizz Scale

5	Run away!
4	Crying
3	Heart beating fast
2	Face feels hot
1	Butterflies in my belly
0	I'm okay

Fizz

While the rats ate lunch around the school campfire, Lucy couldn't stop worrying about the tunnel which was making her Fizz levels go higher and higher. She really wanted to go home, but she also wanted to get a special medal from Mr Chip at the end of the obstacle course!

Lucy decided to move away from the campfire and try to concentrate on the **Right Now** skill. Right Now, Lucy could **see** a bird in a tree, some ants crawling on a wooden plank, a ladybird on a leaf, some water in a pond and her friend sneaking an extra marshmallow! Seeing these five things made her smile.

Ha! Ha! Ha! Ha! Ha! Ha!

Marsh

Next, Lucy listened for sounds she could hear in the woods. There were lots of interesting noises, so she listened very carefully. **Right Now,** Lucy could **hear** a busy bee buzzing, a bird singing on a branch, her friends giggling by the campfire and... wait... was that a frog burping? Ewww! Hearing these four things made Lucy giggle.

Finally, Lucy took **one big deep breath** by breathing in through her nose and out through her mouth. She noticed that she wasn't feeling fizzed up anymore and she felt much better. The Right Now skill had helped her think about other things instead of worrying about the tunnel!

Just as Lucy thought about the tunnel she felt a little bit worried again, so she decided to talk to Mr Chip and tell him how she was feeling. Mr Chip smiled warmly at her and said "Lucy, have I ever told you about the **It Will Pass** skill?" Lucy shook her head.

"The **It Will Pass** skill is very helpful when we are feeling scared and want to run away from something that we have to do. Just like you've been feeling about the tunnel. It sounds like you really want to complete the obstacle course but you're a little bit frightened of the tunnel, is that right?" Lucy nodded and Mr Chip reassured her. "It's okay to feel a little bit frightened of something new. Why don't you try going through the tunnel whilst saying to yourself **It Will Pass**. The tunnel isn't very long and you will reach the other end in no time!"

Lucy smiled at Mr Chip and looked at the tunnel. She bravely decided to give it a go - she really wanted that medal! Lucy took another deep breath and crawled into the entrance of the dark tunnel.

Inside the tunnel was gloomy and a bit slimy on Lucy's handss. At first she wanted to turn back but then she remembered Mr Chip saying "**It Will Pass!**" so she thought about the special medal and whispered to herself "I can do this, it will pass!"

One step at a time...

Lucy repeated these words as she moved
through the tunnel bit-by-bit until finally she
could **see** some light shining at the end!
She could **hear** her friends shouting "Go Lucy Go!"
and she could **feel** some mud
tickling her tail – it felt nice!

As she reached the end of the tunnel she could **smell** the fresh air and she popped out with a **big deep breath** and a very big grin. All her friends were cheering and Mr Chip was smiling - Lucy would get her special medal after all!

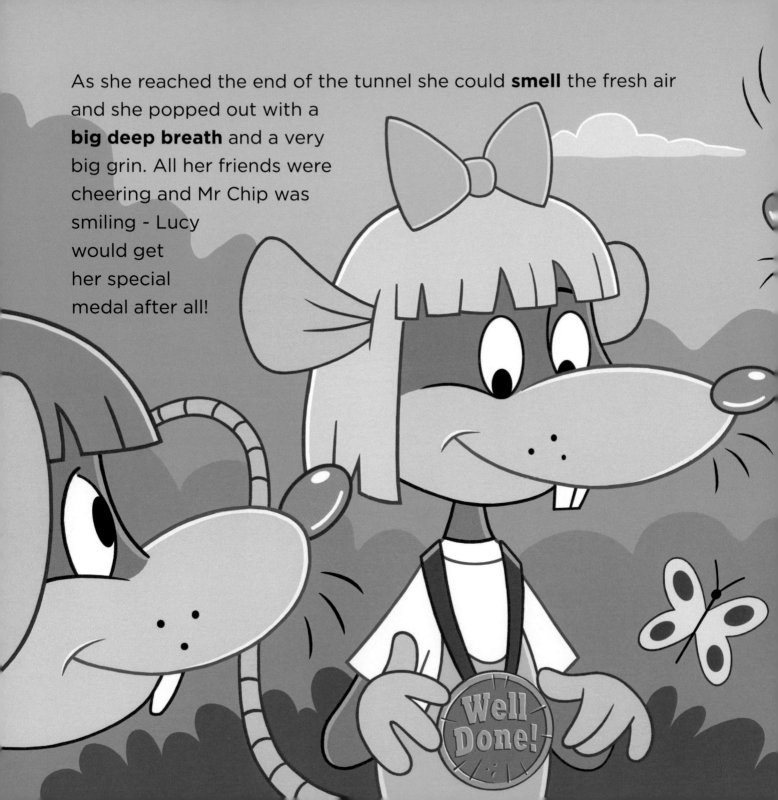

Learning Together : The Fizz

When we feel different emotions like happy, sad, angry or scared,
we can sometimes feel different things happening inside our body.

In the story, Lucy was scared, and she could feel **her heart beating faster** and
butterflies in her belly.

These feelings made her want to run away. This is called **feeling the Fizz**.

If we can learn to notice our Fizz, then we can do things to help lower our Fizz.
Lowering your Fizz can make you feel much better.

In the story, Lucy noticed her Fizz and it helped her to realise that she was feeling
scared. She was so "fizzed-up" that she nearly didn't do the obstacle course.

Lucy's Fizz Scale

5	Run away!
4	Crying
3	Heart beating fast
2	Face feels hot
1	Butterflies in my belly
0	I'm okay

Have a look at the Fizz bottle and see if you can describe your own Fizz when you feel scared about something.

You can ask an adult to help you! 0 = feeling okay and 5 = feeling fizzed-up.

Your Fizz scale when you feel scared

5	
4	
3	
2	
1	
0	

Questions to ask and talk about together

Question 1: In the woods, what made Lucy's Fizz go up?

Question 2: If Lucy hadn't used some skills to lower her Fizz what do you think might have happened?

The It Will Pass Skill

The It Will Pass skill helps us to get through situations that make us feel upset, scared or want to run away. We can do something if we know that It Will Pass!

In the story, Lucy really wanted to get the special medal but she didn't want to go into the tunnel. In the end she calmed down and went through the tunnel and was very proud of herself for being so brave!

She realised that the tunnel wasn't that scary after all!

Questions to ask and talk about together

Question 1: Can you think of a time when you felt the same as Lucy but you were able to be brave and do the thing that made you feel scared?

Question 2: How did it make you feel?

Question 3: What helped you to do it?

Question 4: How did you feel afterwards?

The Right Now Skill

5 4 3 2 1

The Right Now skill helps us to stay focused on the here and now instead of worrying about things that have happened in the past or may happen in the future.

Let's practice Right Now!

5	Things you can **see** right now?
4	Things you can **hear** right now?
3	Things you can **touch** right now?
2	Things you can **smell** (or taste) right now?
1	And finally, take **1 big deep breath**

Questions to ask and talk about together

Question 1: What did you notice?

Right Now... Get Creative!

The Right Now skill is a fantastic grounding technique and can be used in a variety of settings in a number of different ways.

Note to adults

You could think of your own way to use the Right Now skill! Instead of using the example on the previous page, the 5-4-3-2-1 could be:

5 star jumps, 4 hops, 3 claps, 2 touch your toes and 1 big deep breath or whatever you think will suit the needs of the child in that moment.

Get creative and make it fun!
The key is to make sure you encourage the use of different senses and you can even introduce movement!

Rat Fact
Rats giggle when they are tickled but the sound is at such a high frequency that we can't hear it!

Rat Fact
A group of Rats is called a Mischief!

Get The Decider Skills App!

Further information about The Decider Skills used in this book can be found at **www.getselfhelp.co.uk** You can also download **The Decider Skills STOPP App** for your mobile phone!